A Newbies Guide to Final Cut Pro X 10.2:

A Beginnings Guide to Video Editing Like a Pro

Minute Help Guides

Minute Help Press

www.minutehelp.com

Table of Contents

Introduction

Are you ready to get serious about digital video editing? Apple's famous video editing software Final Cut Pro X is just the tool for the job. Final Cut Pro X, or FCPX, is an incredibly powerful editing solution that gives you complete control over your footage, audio, title sequences and much more. In fact, it's something of a film industry standard at the professional level.

Don't be intimidated by FCPX's pedigree though. Apple is famous for intuitive software that's friendly to novices and power users alike, and FCPX is no different. With a little bit of practice, you'll quickly find that you're more than capable of mastering FCPX's extensive range of features – features that will help you immensely in the lifelong journey of mastering your craft as a filmmaker!

This guide was written for newbies and seasoned editors alike. With that said, a word of caution: FCPX is a professional-class piece of software, meaning it's designed to be as feature-rich as possible. This necessarily means that its interface requires a little more attention than simpler, consumer-centric platforms do – it's not the kind of thing you can install and figure out at a glance.

Nevertheless, we think you'll find that FCPX surprisingly easy to use, especially given its scope. With a little bit of dedication, you'll get the hang of things quickly. Of course, we'll be there to help you along the way, with lots of tips, tricks, screenshots and tutorials to get you up and running.

In **Chapter 1: Getting to Know Final Cut Pro X**, we'll introduce you to FCPX with a quick tour of its basic elements. Next, in **Chapter 2: Importing and Managing Media,** we'll help you get started with the building blocks of your project. In **Chapter 3: Basic Editing,** you'll learn how to put together your first project, along with some basic editing techniques. **Chapter 4: Titles, Music and Sound, Transitions, Effects and More** gives you the scoop on all of the extras that make the difference between a rough cut and a professional product. In **Chapter 5: Advanced Editing,** we'll explore some higher level editing functions, like secondary storylines, color correction and audio equalization. Finally, in **Chapter 6: FCPX and Beyond**, we'll share some incredible paid and free resources and extensions for FCPX, including Apple's Motion and Compressor.

Ready to take your first steps toward that Academy Award? Read on to get started with Final Cut Pro X!

Chapter 1: Getting to Know Final Cut Pro

In this chapter, we're going to get you on your feet in FCPX by giving you a quick overview of the software, helping you through the installation process and introducing you to the major elements of the interface (windows, menus, playback controls and shortcuts). There's a lot of information here, but with a platform as complex as FCPX, we think having a solid foundation in the basics will save you tons of time and frustration as you delve deeper into FCPX's capabilities.

1.1 Final Cut Pro in a Nutshell

So what exactly can you do with Final Cut Pro X? Glad you asked! FCPX gives you everything you need to realize your vision, with editing tools designed to help you wrangle your video, audio and title clips into a coherent vision.

Final Cut Pro X is a perfect tool for an amateur filmmaker, but make no mistake: the pros use this too. Quite a few major films were edited using earlier versions of this software, including *John Carter* (2012), *True Grit* (2010) and *The Girl with the Dragon Tattoo* (2011). FCPX can be as simple or as complex as your needs as a filmmaker. It's equally capable of stitching together your kids' school plays for a commemorative family disc as it is of manipulating green screen footage and managing multiple camera angles and audio channels. FCPX will handle most video, image and audio formats, and version 10.2 adds support for

More specifically, FCPX is a storyline-based editor. It's organized around your primary storyline. That storyline provides the spine of a FCPX project – all of your titles, transitions, background music, and audio tracks support that spine. In other words, FCPX is designed for storytelling. Rather than plopping clips and audio into a linear track, FCPX gives you the freedom to rearrange your Timeline fluidly and logically according to narrative logic. It also provides excellent solutions for media management, thanks to its robust organizational features, so you can find and reuse footage easily. Not only does FCPX make it easy to arrange your footage, it also gives you powerful editing tools to manage color, effects, transitions, audio balance, and much, much more.

Bear in mind that this kind of power requires a pretty powerful machine. You'll need a Mac running OS X 10.10.2 (Yosemite) or later, with at least 4 GB of RAM and 256 MB of VRAM (more is better, particularly if you plan to do a lot of work with 3D titles). You'll also need an OpenCL-compatible graphics card and at least 4.15 GB of disk space.

We think you'll get a much clearer picture of what FCPX is and how it works by rolling up your sleeves and diving in, so in that spirit, let's download the software and start poking around.

1.2 Downloading Final Cut Pro X

The very first thing you'll need to do to get started with Final Cut Pro X is to download it. Final Cut Pro X is available for $299.99 in the Apple App Store or through the Apple site at https://www.apple.com/final-cut-pro/. On the Apple site, you can download the full version using the **Buy Now** button in the top right corner, or you can click **Free Trial** to test drive FCPX for thirty days. The trial is a great way to see if the software is a good fit for you – no credit card is required.

Final Cut Pro X   What's New   What is Final Cut Pro?   In Action   Resources   Tech Specs   Free Trial   Buy Now

Try Final Cut Pro X free for 30 days.

To get a free trial of Final Cut Pro X version 10.2 for your Mac, enter your name
and email address in the box below, then click Download.

First Name (Required)

Last Name (Required)

Email Address (Required)

Apple Privacy Policy

☑ Keep me up to date with Apple news, software updates,
and the latest information on products and services.

Location
⊙ United States
○ Other
Why do we need this?

Download free trial

If you're using a previous version of the Final Cut Pro X trial, you'll be able
to use this version free for an additional 30 days.

Final Cut Pro X requires a Mac with OS X v10.10.2 or later, 4GB of RAM
(8GB recommended for 4K editing and 3D titles), and an OpenCL-capable
graphics card or Intel HD Graphics 3000 or later. For details, see
minimum system requirements.

Screenshot 1: The Final Cut Pro X Free Trial Download Screen

Once you've downloaded FCPX, follow the prompts to install it. If you've purchased the full version, most of your work should be done for you thanks to the magic of Mac. If you downloaded the trial, you'll need to double click on the downloaded installer file. You'll then be walked through the steps of getting FCPX up and running.

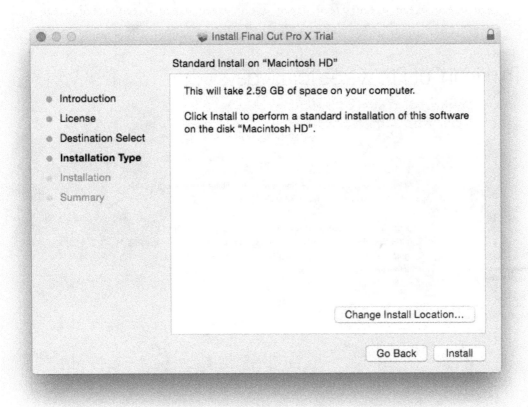

Screenshot 2: Installing FCPX Trial Version

Once you've clicked through the installation assistant, Final Cut Pro X will open. If it doesn't, use Spotlight Search, Launchpad or your Applications folder to find it and open it.

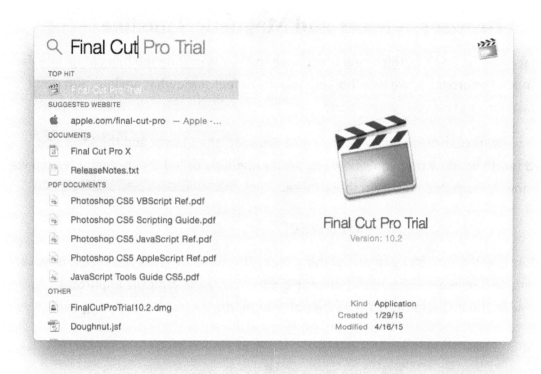

Screenshot 3: Searching for FCPX using Spotlight

Once you've opened FCPX for the first time, you should see something like this:

Screenshot 4: Final Cut Pro X

If it seems inscrutable at first, don't worry! We'll help you find your way around in the next section!

1.3 Browser, Viewer and Magnetic Timeline

One of the toughest Final Cut Pro X hurdles new users have to clear is getting the hang of its interface. The first time you open the program, we won't blame you if you feel somewhat anxious. But don't worry! It doesn't take long to find your way around.

The FCPX interface consists of three major windows – the Browser, the Viewer and the Magnetic Timeline. There's a fourth window that you'll be using pretty regularly called the Inspector, which we'll cover shortly. For now, though, let's focus on these three.

Browser

The Browser window is in the top left quadrant of the screen. This window gives you access to your FCPX libraries, events and keyword collections (Chapter 2 will cover these critically important concepts). The Browser also includes thumbnail views of your media for quick previewing and prepping.

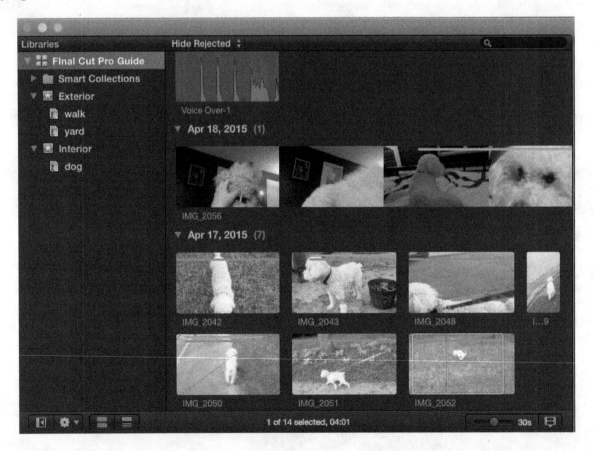

Screenshot 5: Browser

You can adjust the interface itself to suit your viewing needs as you go. Use your mouse to make windows larger or smaller. You can also hide and reveal the Inspector for more screen space as needed.

Viewer

The Viewer is a playback tool that sits next to the Browser. The Viewer displays whatever frame is currently active, either from the files in the Browser window or from the current project on your Magnetic Timeline.

Screenshot 6: Viewer

The Viewer window can be viewed in full screen using the full screen button in its lower right corner. Use the percentage in the top right corner to zoom in or out, and use the arrows and play button in the center to control playback.

If you're having trouble wrapping your head around the Viewer's dual function as a playback tool for your raw files in the Browser and your managed masterpiece in the Magnetic Timeline (or if you'd just like to have two Viewer windows open), you can turn on the Event Viewer by clicking **Window > Show Event Viewer** in the top menu bar. This will open a second Viewer window, and you'll be able to view previews of both unedited clips in the Browser and processed footage in the Timeline.

Magnetic Timeline

The Magnetic Timeline houses your FCPX project as you create and perfect it. This is where the magic of FCPX really happens! The Magnetic Timeline's magnetism refers to the fact that clips placed on the Timeline are "magnetized" to each other. If you remove a clip, its neighbors are pulled toward each other, so you don't have to manually readjust them. Similarly, if you move a clip between two other clips, everything will rearrange itself to accommodate the clip's new position.

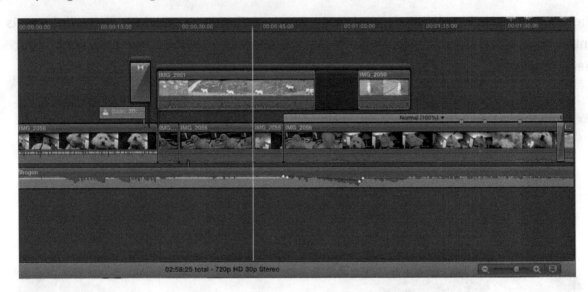

Screenshot 7: Magnetic Timeline

Your Timeline includes your primary storyline in the main track in the middle of the project space. It also includes any secondary storylines, audio tracks, connected clips, titles or transitions you may have added.

You can adjust your Timeline's appearance by using the zoom tool in the lower right corner. Next to the zoom slider, you'll also see the tiny **Clip Appearance** button. Click it to choose between a few different options for viewing your clips. The default view shows large video frames with audio tracks underneath, though you can choose to view audio only (the first option) or video only (the fifth option).

Screenshot 8: Clip Appearance

As you begin editing, you'll find yourself zooming in and out of your Timeline quite regularly. We've found that the keyboard shortcut COMMAND + + (hold the COMMAND key while pressing the + key) is much easier to use than the slider at the bottom. You can also press SHIFT + Z at any time to cause your entire project to appear within the Timeline.

Timeline Index

You'll find a button at the very bottom left corner of the FCPX screen called the Timeline Index. This button will reveal a list of everything that's included in your project. You can use the tabs at the bottom to view video, audio and transition files by themselves as well.

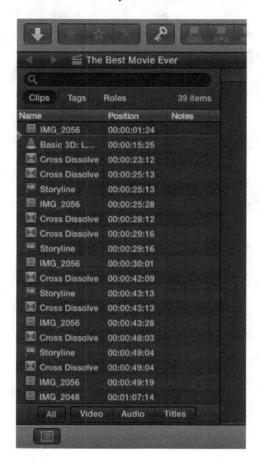

Screenshot 9: Timeline Index

In a big project, this can be a great way to find clips using the search tool at the top. You can also click on an asset here to cause the playhead to jump to that point in the Timeline.

Meter

You'll find a very important tool in the very middle of the row that separates the Timeline from the Browser and the Viewer. The meter displays the time of the video and the decibel level of the audio.

Screenshot 10: Meter

1.4 Inspector

A fourth and equally important panel – the Inspector – will only appear once you've got media imported and a project started. This panel will change depending on where your playhead is. At the top, you'll see that you can inspect the properties of Video, Audio and Info.

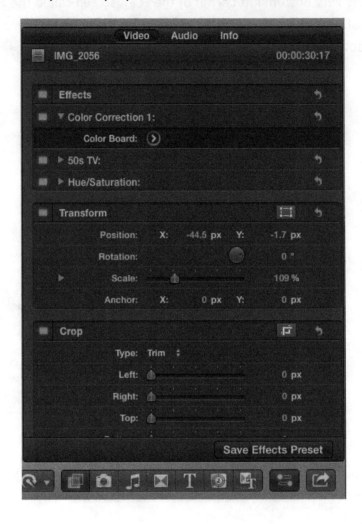

Screenshot 11: Inspector

The Inspector panel will allow you to add effects and much, much more. You can hide and unhide the Inspector panel by clicking its icon. We'll be referring to the Inspector frequently throughout this guide, since it's where you can make some of the most important video and audio customizations.

Screenshot 12: Inspector Icon

1.4 FCPX Menus and Buttons

When you first start using FCPX, it can feel like there's a menu set and button row jammed into every nook and cranny of the software. It may take a while to get a feel for the location of every single feature, but keep in mind that menus tend to be logically grouped. Global functions can be found in the very top Apple menu. Media management functions are found near the Browser, and tools for moving clips between the Browser and the Timeline are located between those two windows.

If you can't find something, the **Help** menu at the top of your Mac's screen can be very useful. Type the menu item you need, and FCPX will find it for you and show you where it is.

Screenshot 13: Finding Trim End Using the Help Menu

You can tell if a feature represented by a button is active by its color. Inactive buttons are white; active buttons are blue. Most buttons (though not all) is duplicated in the FCPX menu.

1.5 Playback

One of the most important and most movable elements of FCPX is the playhead. This is the strong white vertical line that appears over your project in the Timeline. By default, video skimming will be enabled in FCPX, meaning you'll see a second red line called the skimmer. The skimmer can be used to preview clips in the Browser or other parts of the Timeline without moving the playhead and losing your spot.

Screenshot 14: Playhead and Skimmer

Any time you want to play something in FCPX – whether it's your project, an event in your library, or an audio sample – press the spacebar to begin playback. Press it again to end playback. Playback will be based on wherever your playhead or skimmer is when you press the spacebar.

While the space bar is the quickest way to pause and play video based on the location of the playhead or skimmer, you can also use **J** (reverse playback), **K** (normal playback) and **L** (pause) as more precise tools for getting around inside your clips. You can also hold down **K** and press **J** and **L** to play your clip in slow motion. This is incredibly useful for finding specific points for making cuts or edits in your footage.

If you want to play an entire selected clip, select the clip by clicking on it and then press the **/** key.

You can move through your clips on your Timeline using the up and down arrows. It's a little counter-intuitive to press up to move back toward the left edge of the screen, but it's a useful way to get around your Timeline.

The **Play Around** tool is also very helpful in quickly checking your edits as you make them. To use it, click **View > Playback > Play Around** or press **SHIFT + ?.** By default, this will play the two seconds before and the two seconds after the position of your playhead. You can adjust this in Preferences if you need to. It's a handy way to test transitions and other edits.

Snapping

The snapping feature makes it much easier to navigate your Timeline. If your playhead is reasonably close to the beginning of a clip, it will "snap" to the start of that clip if snapping is enabled. You'll find the snapping button at the very far right just above your Magnetic Timeline, and you can also turn it on or off by pressing **N.**

Audio and Video Skimming

Audio skimming is incredibly useful when you're editing based on audio – for example, a particularly juicy sound bite from an interview. It gives you scrubbed audio as you move your mouse across a clip. On the other hand, if you're *not* editing for audio, audio skimming can be extremely grating. Turn it on or off using the button next to the snapping button above your Magnetic Timeline or by pressing **SHIFT+S.**

You can also turn full skimming (video and audio) on and off using the button to the left of the audio skimming button or by pressing **S.** Video skimming creates a second line in your Timeline. Your playhead remains stationary, while the red skimmer line can be moved by moving your cursor when skimming is active. With skimming turned off, you'll need to click to move to a different point in your Timeline.

Playback Preferences

One of the most important things in the playback preferences area (**Final Cut Pro > Preferences > Playback**) is the automatic rendering setting. Rendering is what happens every time you add a new clip, effect, transition, or other alteration. Older versions of the software required you to manually render your shots. Fortunately, FCPX will automatically handle rendering as soon as you stop working.

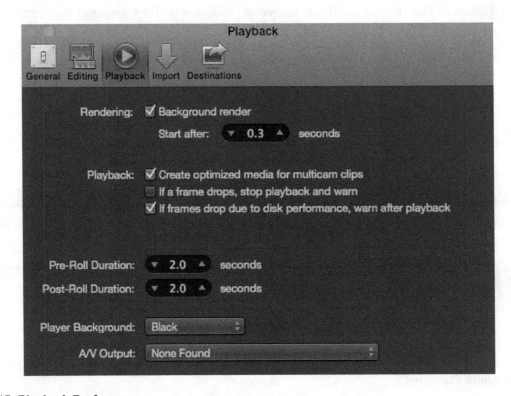

Screenshot 17: Playback Preferences

Background render should be checked by default. You may want to adjust the length of time FCPX will wait before starting an automatic render according to your system's needs.

1.6 Keyboard Shortcuts

FCPX includes a vast array of keyboard shortcuts that eliminate the need to go hunting through menu nests with your mouse. Learning to use shortcuts will make your post processing significantly faster, but it's easy to get overwhelmed in the beginning. Fortunately, there's only one shortcut you *really* need to memorize – COMMAND + OPTION + K. Pressing these three keys will bring up a keyboard map that details all of FCPX's shortcuts.

Screenshot 18: Keyboard Shortcuts in FCPX

Clicking on each key will reveal all of the shortcuts it's associated with. You can also search using the search tool in the top right corner.

We'll clue you in on common shortcuts as we go through this guide. For your convenience, shortcuts are also listed next to their associated menu items in the FCPX software, as shown below in the **Mark** menu.

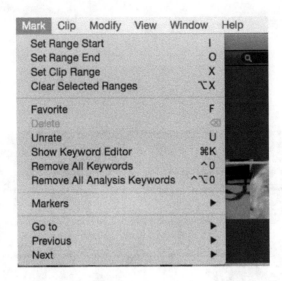

Screenshot 19: Keyboard Shortcuts in Menus

If you find yourself navigating to a particular menu item often, we recommend trying to learn its shortcut. Note that many FCPX shortcuts are single key shortcuts, like F for Favorite. Many make some pneumonic sense, like T for Trim, but not all of them!

Editing Keyboard Shortcuts

As you get used to FCPX, you may come across the occasional command that doesn't have a keyboard shortcut. You may also wish that a particular command had a *different* shortcut. Fortunately, you can customize your shortcuts and add new ones as needed. To do so, open the Command Editor by pressing COMMAND + OPTION + K.

To set up your own shortcuts, click **Default** in the top left corner of the Command Editor and then click **Duplicate.** Give your customized shortcut group a name. Then, search for the command you want to edit using the search box in the top right corner of the Command Editor. When you find the command you need, just drag it to the main key you want to associate it with. You can then choose modifier keys as needed.

Chapter 2: Importing and Managing Media

We know that you're itching to get started editing, but first you'll need to learn how to gather all of your ingredients. This chapter will show you how to import, organize and search media files in Final Cut Pro X.

It's incredibly easy to import video, stills and audio into FCPX, and we think that its organizational tools are some of the best in the business. Trust us – a little attention to your media organizational structure now will pay off in a big way in the future!

2.1 Importing Media

To get started with your first FCPX project, you'll need some source files. These might be stored on your iPhone/iPad, your computer, your video camera, or some other device or storage platform. Fortunately, FCPX makes it easy to import files from a variety of sources. To get started, click the **Import Media** icon in the Browser window, or click **File > Import > Media** in the main toolbar.

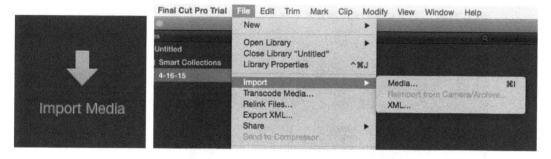

Screenshot 20: Importing Media

If your media files are already on your computer or a connected external drive, go ahead and find them by using the file navigation at the bottom of the screen. Keep in mind that if your source files are stored in iPhoto or iMovie, you'll need to export them from those programs in order to be able to get to them through FCPX using this method.

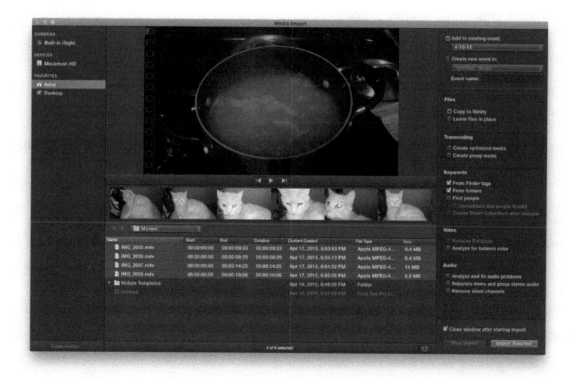

Screenshot 21: Importing Four Video Files from Our Computer

Note that when you import media, you can keep things organized by adding your files to existing events or by creating new events. This can be a great way to keep track of projects, scenes or other groupings of your media.

Screenshot 22: Creating a New Event

By default, FCPX will copy the files into your library, leaving your existing media files exactly where you left them. This is a great way to be sure that your originals stay safe, but if you're concerned about disk space, you can also move files instead of copying them.

When you're ready, click **Import** to start the process.

If you have footage on a camera, plug in your camera to your Mac. FCPX should discover the device and walk you through the process of importing directly from it.

If your videos are stored in iMovie or iPhoto/Photos, check out 4.7 to learn how to skip the importation process altogether!

Import Settings

The import settings area includes basic import preferences. This is where you can decide whether to copy your source files or work with them from their original locations. You can also manage your keyword settings here. There are a few enhancement options for audio and video as well. Checking them will give you a little bit of automatic post processing, though in general we'd recommend taking a more hands-on approach.

Screenshot 23: Import Settings

2.2 Events, Libraries and Folders

If you've used iPhoto or iMovie, you may be familiar with the concept of an import "event." Events are simply ways of grouping your media files. They can keep your source material organized by import date or any metric of your choosing. You can rename events by clicking them and then clicking again, so that your cursor appears. Then delete and type as necessary.

You can organize events into "libraries." You'll find your libraries in the Browser window, where you can rename them by clicking them to select them. Then click again to activate your cursor. To create a new library, simply click **File > New > Library**. As you start building up projects, libraries can be immensely helpful in keeping everything organized! When you create a new library, you can choose the location for the library. We generally recommend using some sort of external storage, because video files will eat up hard drive space at an unbelievable rate.

You can also copy events from one library to another. Just drag the event you want to copy to the destination library. Note that this is a copy operation, not a move.

Libraries can be disconnected and then opened again. To remove a library from FCPX (but not from your computer), right click the library and then click **Close Library**. To reopen it, click **File > Open Library**. As you start accumulating footage and projects, this can help keep the FCPX Browser tidy. It's also useful for libraries containing footage stored on a removable drive.

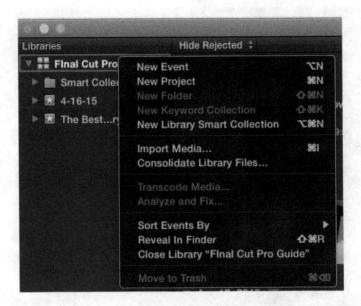

Screenshot 24: Closing a Library

It is also possible to organize your clips into folders, which, unlike keyword collections (discussed later on in 2.5), can be nested inside each other. Create a new folder inside an FCPX event by clicking **File > New > New Folder** or by pressing COMMAND + SHIFT + N.

2.3 Files, Clips and Projects

Before you get much further, you'll want to be very clear on the difference between files, clips and projects. Your media files – video, audio and graphics – are your raw source material. You include pieces of these files ("clips") in a FCPX "project." The project doesn't actually alter the files themselves, but rather points to specific bits of information in those files as you edit. "Clips" represent those bits. The great thing about this setup is that FCPX doesn't alter your original media. This gives you freedom to play around as you edit without being afraid of losing precious footage!

You can copy clips to other events and libraries by simply dragging them from the Browser to the event you'd like to copy to. This won't move the clips from their original location, but it will copy the files and all of their metadata. To actually move a clip from one place to another, click on it to select it (or COMMAND + CLICK to select multiple clips). Then click **File > Move Clips to Library** and then choose the destination library.

You can view your clips in filmstrip view or in list view. Filmstrip view provides thumbnails of each clip, but list view gives you quite a bit more information. Use the View buttons beneath the Browser to switch between the two.

Screenshot 25: Clip View Buttons

List view shows several columns of information, and you're not limited to the default columns.

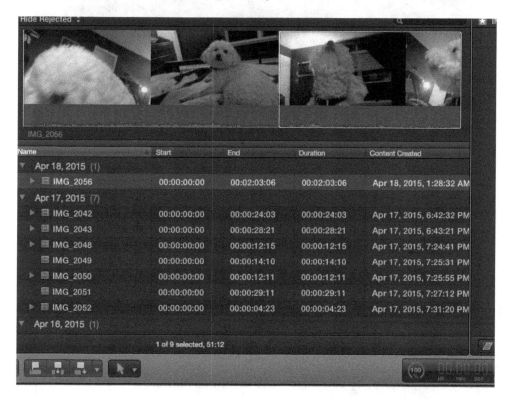

Screenshot 26: List View

Just right click on the column headers to see every other available column, and select additional columns to display by clicking on them as needed.

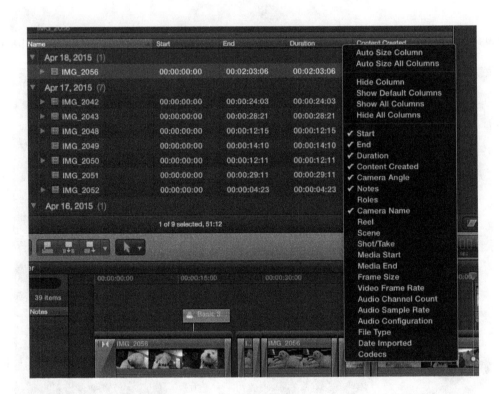

Screenshot 27: Selecting Columns in List View

You can then sort by each column by clicking on the column's name.

2.4 Grouping, Favoriting and Rejecting Clips

When you build up a large library of source files, FCPX's grouping and rating tools come in handy as you sift through takes. When viewing clips, you can choose to view grouped clips or to sort clips, as shown below.

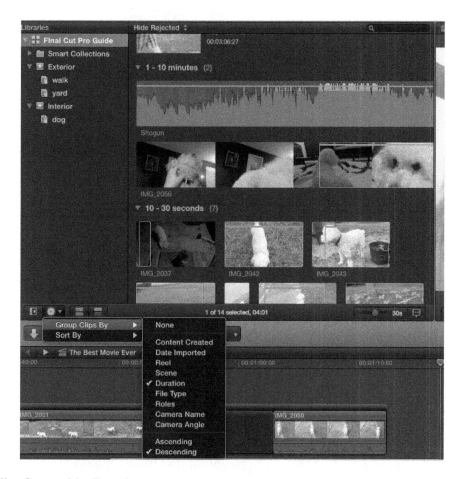

Screenshot 28: Clips Grouped by Duration

Grouping can be very useful when you're dealing with a large volume of clips, since you can collapse each group as needed. You can also change the order of the groups by choosing **Ascending** and **Descending.** If you sort your clips instead of grouping them, you won't see headings.

To rate your clips, select a clip and use the green star to favorite it (or press **F**), the hollow star to remove the favorite, and the x to reject the clip. Rejecting a clip won't delete the clip, but you can hide it from view by clicking the arrows in the top left corner of the Browser window and then clicking **Hide Rejected.**

Screenshot 29: Tools for Rating Footage in FCPX

When you favorite a clip, a green line will appear across its thumbnail image to make it easy to quickly identify your best shots.

Screenshot 30: A Favorited Portion of a Clip

2.5 Keyword Collections

In FCPX, keyword collections function as organizational elements as well as handy searching tools. Your keyword collections will appear in your Browser, somewhat like folders in Finder. To assign a keyword to a clip, click on it to select it and then click the keyword icon underneath the Browser or press COMMAND + K.

Screenshot 31: Keyword Icon

You can actually import folder names as keywords when importing media. Doing this will preserve each folder name as a keyword, which can help you keep your initial media file organization scheme intact.

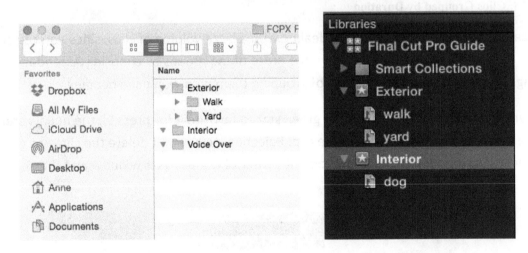

Screenshot 32: Folder Names and Keywords

You can also assign keyboard shortcuts to your most frequently used keywords in the keyword dialog box to speed up the process of adding keywords after importing files. You can add multiple keywords to a single clip, though this will mean that the clip will appear in multiple keyword collections.

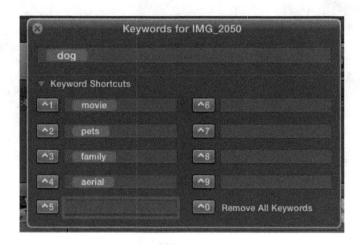

Screenshot 33: Keyword Shortcuts

You can add a keyword to an entire clip, or mark a portion of a clip (see 3.2) and add a keyword to that. A clip that is associated with a keyword collection will display a blue line in its thumbnail image, as shown below.

Screenshot 34: A Clip with Associated Keywords

You can delete a keyword collection by right clicking the keyword in the Browser and then clicking **Delete Keyword Collection.** This won't delete your clips – only the keyword associated with them.

2.6 Searching Footage and Using Smart Collections

In FCPX, you can search for file names in the search field in the top right corner of the Browser. This can be helpful if you have an extremely good memory for file names. Fortunately, you can access more detailed search settings by clicking the magnifying glass next to the search field. This brings up a more sophisticated filter-building screen.

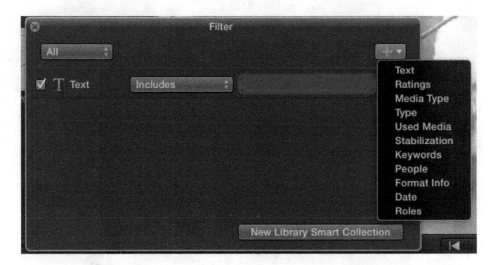

Using this tool, you can add criteria like keyword, media type, date, etc. to the search by clicking the plus sign. To remove criteria, click the check box to deselect items. You can also choose to search for files that include your search term, or you can search for files that do *not* include that term. Alternatively, you can use the *is* and *is not* filters to look for exact matches. For example, you could perform a search for every video file that contains the letters IMG shot on December 24, 2014 that you've favorited.

A powerful feature related to FCPX's search abilities is its Smart Collection feature. A Smart Collection is a saved search. By clicking **New Library Smart Collection**, you can save your search and expect FCPX to update it as you add new footage and/or tweak your keywords and favorites.

Chapter 3: Basic Editing

Now that you've got some media imported and organized in Final Cut Pro X, it's time to start putting it together in your first FCPX project! In this chapter, we'll cover the basics of FCPX project creation and editing.

3.1 Creating Your First Project

To create a new project, simply click **New Project** in the Timeline window, click **File > New > New Project,** or press COMMAND + N.

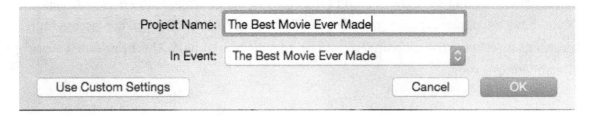

Screenshot 36: Creating a New Project

Give your project a name and choose the event you'd like to associate it with, and you're all set!

Saving a Project

It may take some getting used to, but FCPX doesn't have a Save button. Your project is saved automatically as you work, so you never have to worry about power loss or computer lockups causing you to lose all of your hard work!

3.2 Marking Clips

You'll probably want to mark your clips before adding them to your Timeline. Marking clips simply means that you set a start point and an end point inside the clip, which then becomes an insertable clip itself. To do this, move your mouse over the file's thumbnail in the Browser window. You'll see a red line appear. To get really specific, use the arrow keys to nudge forward and backward. When you do this, you'll see a yellow line that represents your entry point, and the red line will follow the mouse as you define the clip's end point.

Screenshot 37: Marking a Clip

When you've found your starting point, tap the **I** key on the keyboard ("I" for "In"). You can also use the top toolbar and click **Mark > Set Range Start,** but we think it's easier to keep your place if you use the keyboard shortcuts.

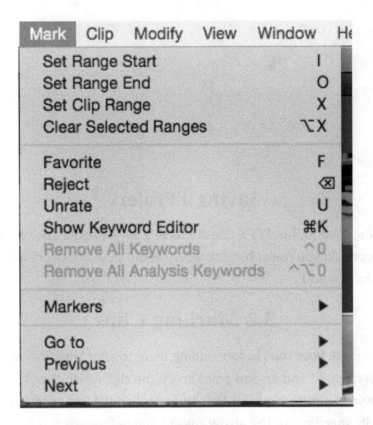

Screenshot 38: Marking Range Starts in the Menu

Now that you've got your starting point, find your end point using your mouse and the arrow keys again. Mark the end point by pressing the **O** key on the keyboard. Congratulations – you've just marked your first clip!

Reviewing your footage and breaking out the bits that you like and want to include using **I** and **O** and then marking favorites and rejecting bad apples will make adding clips to your storyline move much faster. It's also a great way to get your footage organized and develop a good working idea of your project's shape before you start actually editing.

3.3 Adding Clips to the Primary Storyline

Once you've defined some clips, as described above, it's time to actually drop them into your developing film project. You can drag and drop clips from the Browser into the Timeline, or you can use the three buttons located at the bottom of the Browser window:

Screenshot 39: Adding Clips

The first button inserts the clip as a connected clip (more on this in 5.1). The second inserts the clip in between two clips at the location of the playhead, and the third tacks it on at the end of the project. You can use the keyboard letters Q, W, and E respectively to do these tasks, and we think it makes the process go a lot faster!

Video and Audio Only Insertion

Clicking the arrow next to the insertion buttons pictured above will give you the option to add video or audio only from a file. This is a great way to get rid of background noise straight out of the gate. You can also use this as a way to add audio from a clip to your project and then play a different video clip on top of it.

3.4 Editing Modes

FCPX includes seven different editing modes, with their respective shortcuts listed in parentheses – Select (A), Trim (T), Position (P), Range Selection (R), Blade (B), Zoom (Z) and Hand (H). Most of the time, you'll probably work in the default mode – Select – but there are circumstances in which your other options will come in handy.

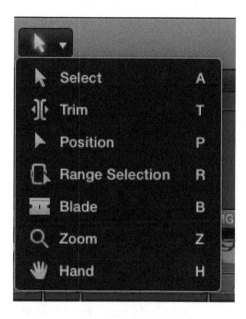

Screenshot 40: FCPX Editing Modes

Trim

To trim a clip in the Timeline, select the Trim tool from the tools menu, or press T. This will cause the mouse cursor to change to a line with arrows pointing in either direction. Clicking and dragging on a clip's edge in either direction will adjust the length of the clip. It's a good way to delete extra bits and pieces of a scene to make things flow smoothly.

Position

Clicking Position or pressing P will allow you to drag clips around on the Timeline without making automatic changes to the position of its surrounding clips. In Position Mode, wherever you drop a clip is where it will stay.

This is great for inserting scenes or titles between existing shots. Using the Position tool, you can even create blank space between shots as in the screenshot below.

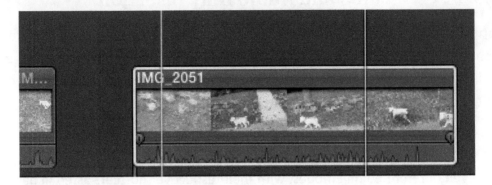

Screenshot 41: Positioning a Clip to Make Room for a Title

You can also nudge a clip to the left or right one frame at a time using the comma key (nudges left) and the period key (nudges right). Adding the SHIFT key to both operations will cause the clip to be nudged ten frames left or right.

Range Selection

The Range Selection tool is great for editing a portion of your Timeline. Use it to select a range of your project for editing. This is essentially what you do when marking clips, but the Range Selection mode setting provides a more visual version of the tool.

Blade

The Blade tool allows you to chop up your clips. Use it to cut a shot in two for repositioning, editing or whatever you need. Just press B or click on the blade tool to use it.

Zoom

The Zoom key (press Z or click the tool) doesn't do quite the same thing that most zoom functions do in other kinds of software. Instead of zooming in on the video images themselves, the zoom key zooms in on the Timeline, making it easier to see each individual frame. This is a really good way to zero in on your project's frames in order to trim or to use the blade tool, since you can see exactly where the cut is going to happen.

Screenshot 42: Zoomed-In Timeline

You can also zoom in and out on the Timeline by using the slider in the bottom right corner of the screen.

Screenshot 43: Zoom Slider

Hand Tool

The hand tool (press H or click the tool) gives you the ability to scroll through the Timeline, though chances are if you're running FCPX 10.2, you're using a well-appointed Mac with a multitouch trackpad! In our opinion, it's easier to scroll using two fingers than it is to activate the hand tool. If for some reason you're trackpad-less, though, the hand tool may be able to help you navigate.

3.5 Basic Editing Methods

In this section, we'll cover the four basic kinds of edits you can perform in FCPX – ripple, roll, slip and slide edits.

Ripple Edits

A ripple edit is the most basic and intuitive kind of edit you'll perform in FCPX. In Select mode (A), move your mouse between two clips so that a line with two arrows pointing either direction appears. Click and a yellow bracket will appear on the edge of the clip. From there, you can add and remove frames using the comma and period keys. If you've selected the beginning edge of a clip, the comma will add frames and the period will remove them. The opposite is true on the end edge of the clip.

Ripple edits depend on having some available "handle" before or after your selected clip. These are frames in the original video file that you didn't mark using the I and O keys but are still available for adding in the edit process.

If you need to see how much extra handle you've got to work with in ripple edits, try using the Precision Editor view. To reveal it, double click the centerline between two clips. This will split the display, and you'll see remaining unused footage for each clip.

Screenshot 44: Precision Editor and Available Handle

The great thing about ripple editing is that it doesn't leave any blank gaps between clips. It will affect the duration of your project, though, and can cause problems with keeping things in sync with secondary storylines or audio tracks. Removing frames will move everything after your selected clip back, and adding frames will move everything forward.

Roll Edits

Roll edits are a great way to handle situations where you want to keep the duration of your project intact but need to move the cut between two clips. This is useful for editing the video of a clip but not its audio - for example, when you're editing reaction shots or back and forths between characters.

Roll editing works by allowing you to select the end of one clip and the beginning of the next one while working in trim mode (T). From there, moving both clip edges will simultaneously lengthen one clip and shorten the other. To roll video without rolling audio, right click on the clip and select **Expand audio/video.** This separates the audio and video tracks, making it possible to make a roll edit on one without affecting the other.

Screenshot 45: Roll Editing Video Only

You can also perform a roll edit using the Precision Editor. Just use the slider in the center to roll across one clip and into the next.

Slip Edits

A slip edit changes the content of a shot, but leaves its position and length alone. To perform a slip edit, enter trim mode by clicking it or by pressing **T**. Then, use your mouse to drag the clip forward or backward. This will pull in the footage just before or after the original clip. The clip looks like it's "slipping" along the track.

Slide Edits

A slide edit, on the other hand, changes a shot's position without affecting its length or content. In trim mode (T), hold down the option key and click and drag the clip to slide it along your storyline to its new location.

Top and Tail Edits

You can quickly adjust the beginning and end of a clip by using OPTION + [and OPTION+]. These two commands perform trim start (top) and trim stop (tail) edits. Basically, they'll shorten your clip based on the skimmer line's position. A trim start operation starts the clip at the playhead, and a trim stop operation ends the clip at the skimmer line.

3.6 Removing Footage from the Storyline

There are a few methods for removing footage from your storyline. The simplest delete operation removes a clip and causes the next clips in the sequence to slide back so that there's no dead space, causing the total duration of the project to shorten. On the other hand, pressing SHIFT+DELETE will remove the clip but will leave a gap that you can later fill with other footage. Using this method, the duration of the project will not change.

If you need to remove a portion of footage that encompasses more than one or less than one clip, use **I** and **O** to mark an in and out point first. Then press **Delete** or **SHIFT + DELETE** to remove it.

3.7 Overwriting, Replacing and Auditioning Footage

If you'd like to overwrite a part of your project with another shot, simply select the clip you want to add in the Browser. Then, select the part of your sequence that you'd like to overwrite on your Timeline. Press **D** to overwrite the existing project footage with the selected clip.

If your new clip is longer than the portion of your sequence that you're replacing, FCPX will automatically chop off the extra time from the end of your replacement clip. Pressing **SHIFT + D** will chop off the extra time from the beginning of the clip instead.

Replacing footage is a little different from overwriting it. Overwriting part of your sequence will not change your project's duration. Replacing footage, on the other hand, will remove an entire clip from your storyline and replace it with another one, keeping the replacement clip's original duration. To replace a clip, just drag it from your Browser to your Timeline. A menu of options will then appear, as shown below.

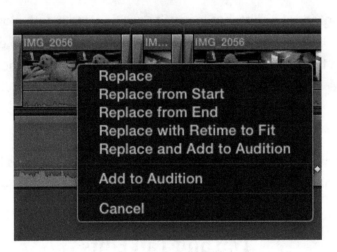

Screenshot 46: Replacing a Clip

The first option – replace – simply swaps out the shots for you. **Replace from Start** and **Replace from End** perform the two overwrite functions previously described. The **Replace with Retime to Fit** will speed up or slow down your replacement clip so that it lasts for the duration of the original but includes every frame of the replacement.

If you're not sure about your replacement, but you'd like to see how it works with your project, choose **Replace and Add to Audition.** This will add a spotlight icon to the clip. Clicking that spotlight will let you choose between the original clip and any audition clips you've added. It's a great way to see what multiple clips look like without losing your original work in case the new clip doesn't work out. You can leave audition clips in place for as long as you like, but if you'd like to finalize your choice, simply right click the clip and then click **Auditions > Finalize Audition.**

3.8 Exporting Your Project

When you're finished with a FCPX project, it's fairly easy to export it so that your intended audience can view it. The easiest way to export is through the Share button, which you'll find about halfway down the right edge of the FCPX screen.

You can use it to save your project on a DVD, optimize it for YouTube, Vimeo, Facebook, or other social destinations, or you can create a "master file." The master file is essentially a single video file that contains your project, and we highly recommend that you create one for every project you complete.

Screenshot 47: Sharing FCPX Projects

At the bottom of the Share menu, you'll see the **Add Destination** option. This will open the FCPX preferences screen.

Screenshot 48: Destinations

Perhaps the most useful thing you'll find here is the **Bundle** folder. A Share Bundle allows you to set up multiple sources for output. For example, you may want to export your project for all Apple devices and for Facebook. Setting up a Bundle Destination can save you a lot of time if you regularly need to export to the same group of services.

Of course, if you're doing very much exporting at all, we highly recommend that you look into Apple's Compressor software (see 6.2). Compressor is an encoding tool that gives you complete control over the encoding of your projects and greatly simplifies the process.

3.9 Practice Makes Perfect

Now that you know the basics of adding clips to your primary storyline and adjusting them to fit your vision, you're well on your way to becoming a successful digital editor. Trimming your clips is a huge component of the art of editing, and we recommend experimenting with FCPX's tools until they become second nature to you. At that point, you can stop worrying about the mechanics of the process and start focusing on developing your editorial style.

Of course, there's much more to editing than trimming. Keep reading to learn all about titles, audio, transitions and special effects that will take your project to the next level!

Chapter 4: Titles, Music and Sound, Transitions, Effects and More

In this chapter, we'll introduce you to the fun stuff! FCPX is an amazing tool for adding everything you need to make your project look professional, and we'll show you all of it here.

Most of the functionality we'll be describing in this chapter is accessible through the line of icons between the Inspector and the Timeline. This row includes several effects browsers. From left to right, you'll find the Enhancements menu, the Retiming menu, Effects, Photos, Music and Sound, Transitions, Titles, Generators and Themes, plus the Inspector toggle and the Share button. These icons contain all kinds of goodies that will help you transform your footage. We'll refer to each one as a browser, but don't confuse them with the Library Browser Window.

Screenshot 49: Effects Icons

4.1 Adding Titles

The T icon gives you the ability to add text to a clip, referred to as a title in the editing world. This is also where you'll find FCPX 10.2's brand new 3D titles!

Screenshot 50: Titles

You can add titles to blank spaces between shots, or drag titles on top of clips to add them to a shot, though some titles cannot be used on top of a shot. The title will appear above the clip as a purple bar on your project's Timeline, as seen below.

Screenshot 51: Viewing a Title on the Timeline

To edit the text of the title, double-click the purple bar. This will activate the title editor in the Inspector panel. Type your text in the Inspector window and preview it in the Viewer.

Screenshot 52: Editing a Title

You'll also find a number of ways to stylize your title. Keep in mind that many of the out-of-the-box title effects are a bit, well, cheesy, and this is especially true of the new 3D options. Don't let this scare you off! With some patience and some good taste, you can easily work with the properties of the title to turn it into something that looks professional!

At the top of the Inspector window, you'll find tabs for Title, Text, Video and Info. The Title tab gives you a few title-specific options, including animation style and the duration of the fade in/out. Text options include font and alignment adjustments. Here you'll also find options for 3D text, including depth, weight and edge style.

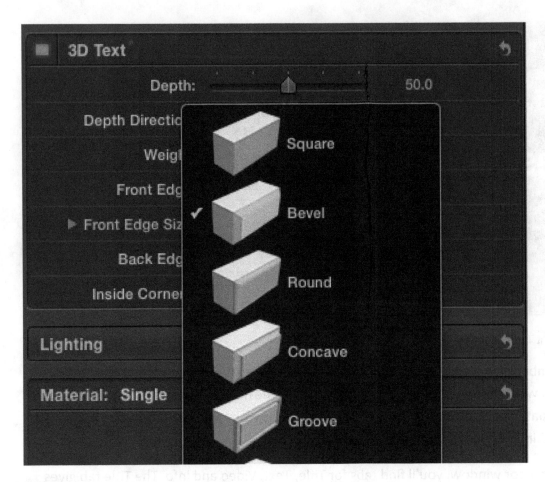

Screenshot 53: 3D Edge Styles

Font preferences also are quite a bit different from choosing a font in a word processing application. The 2D and 3D styles available for use are fairly stylized!

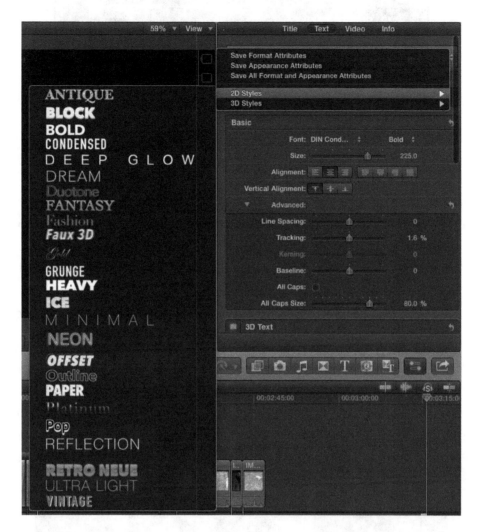

Screenshot 54: 2D Font Styles

Once you've selected a style, you can then (usually) change the actual typeface using the font menu under basic text options. This font menu will include every font that's stored on your computer, including custom or third party fonts you may have.

If you're a typography junkie, you can create your own titles from scratch. Just open the title browser, click **All** on the left, and then click **Custom** on the right to get started.

If you're going to be using titles throughout your project, you may want to save a set of title attributes for use later on. To do this, simply click the text style at the top, and then click **Save All Format and Appearance Attributes.** You can then name your text style and it will be available to you in your style list along with all of FCPX's included styles.

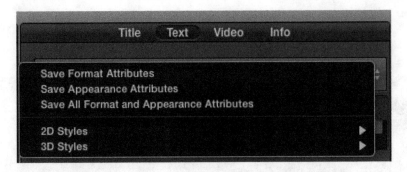

Screenshot 55: Saving a Custom Text Style

Motion Titles

If you're lucky enough to own Apple's Motion 5 3D animation software, you'll find it's an excellent tool for creating gorgeous custom 3D titles. In fact, if you plan on doing much work with titles – 3D or 2D – we *highly* recommend installing Motion. It's easy to import a Motion project into FCPX. Just click **File > Import > Files.** Motion projects will be imported to FCPX as clips, which can be manipulated just like your other clips. Best of all, if you need to edit your Motion project, do so in Motion and FCPX will automatically pick up your changes, so there's no need to reimport. For more about Motion, see 6.1.

4.2 Adding Music and Sound

To add background music, use the music note icon to open the Music and Sound browser. You can access your entire iTunes library here as well (just beware copyright issues if you're making a film for commercial distribution!). You can also easily get to any GarageBand projects you've created. Finally, the iLife Suite (iPhoto, iMovie and GarageBand) includes a sound effects library, which is also accessible here.

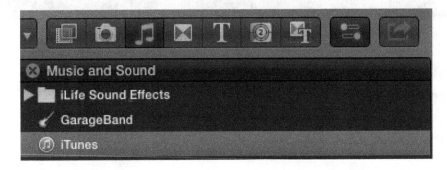

Screenshot 56: Adding Music and Sound

FCPX includes several generic sound effects and music tracks that you can use in your projects. Just drag the effect over to your Timeline to insert it. We'll talk more about fine-tuning your audio in 5.4.

4.3 Adding Transitions

Transitions help smooth the sudden, jarring split between your clips. The Transitions browser is where you'll find dissolving, blurring, moving transitions to stick between your clips to help smooth out your project into a unified piece of work. Transitions are incredibly important in producing a professional piece, though be warned: they're also incredibly easy to overuse!

You can quickly add transitions by clicking the space between two clips and pressing COMMAND + T. This will add a basic dissolve transition between the two clips (you can also select an entire clip and press COMMAND + T to add a transition to both ends of the clip). By default, dissolve transitions last one second. You can drag the edges of this transition to the right or left to make the transition last longer.

To use other transitions and related effects, open up the Transition Browser. You'll see general transition categories on the left and individual transition effects on the right. Find the transition you'd like to use and drag it between two clips on your Timeline to insert it.

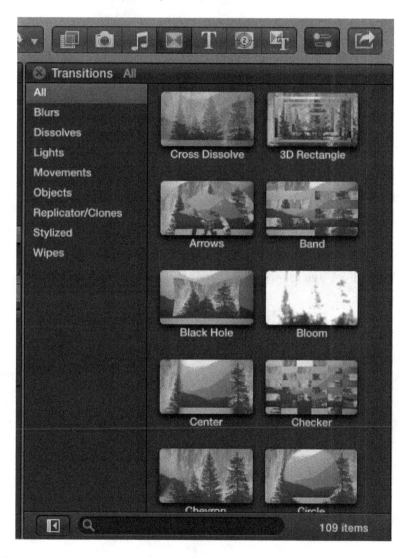

Screenshot 57: Transitions

Once you've applied a transition to a clip, you can slide the gray bars to the right and left to adjust the duration of the transition. For example, in the screenshot below, we've adjusted the transition so that there's a slower dissolve in at the beginning of the clip and a quicker dissolve out.

Screenshot 58: Transitions at the beginning and end of a clip

Some transitions are packaged with configurable options, like color, transparency, etc. To adjust them, select the transition and then open the Inspector, which will display any available transition options.

Note that transitions actually use a handful of frames before and after your clips' start/end points. If you don't have any available frames, you'll be asked if you want to perform a ripple edit, which will shorten your project but will let you insert your transition at your desired location.

4.4 Adding Special Effects

The Effects button opens up several useful video and audio effects options. There are too many to go through here, but it's absolutely worth the time to look through them. Some of them – underwater, night vision, insect eye, etc. – can solve some otherwise tricky filming challenges! To use an effect, drag it from the Effects browser on top of the clip you want to apply it to. You can apply more than one effect to a clip if needed.

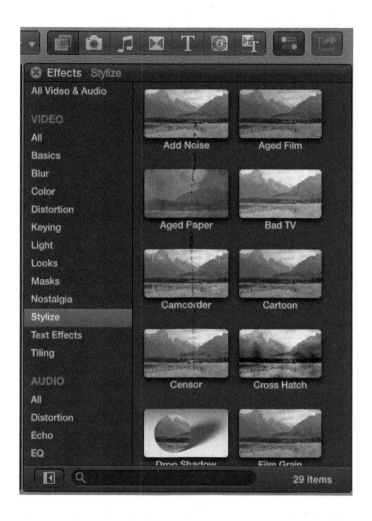

Screenshot 59: Effects

In the Effects browser, you'll also find lots of basic audio effect categories (echo, distortion, etc.). They're added just like video effects, and you can add more than one to a clip. Most audio effects can be heavily manipulated in the Inspector as well.

The Inspector is also useful for turning effects on and off without deleting them. Just click the blue square to turn an effect off for a quick check to be sure that the effect improves your clip. Click that square again to restore it.

Keep in mind that there are plenty of sources for add-on effects – paid and freed. We'll tell you about some of our favorites in Chapter 6.

4.5 Retiming Clips

Retiming gives you the ability to speed your clips up or slow them down (slo mo). The retiming menu above the Timeline gives you everything you need to control the speed of your clip. You can use the **Fast** and **Slow** menus to choose a preselected percentage of change. If you slow a clip down to 50%, it will move at half its normal speed. Setting it to 10% will cause it to move one tenth of its normal speed.

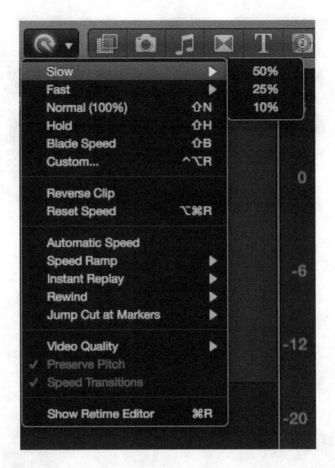

Screenshot 60: Retiming a Clip

For more control, choose **Custom.** Here, you can set any percentage (remember that numbers lower than 100% will slow your clip down and numbers above 100% will speed it up). You can also reverse your film here if you'd like to play the clip backwards.

Screenshot 61: Setting a Custom Speed for a Clip

By default, **Ripple** is checked, which means that changes in the duration of this clip will affect the duration of the whole project. If you uncheck this setting, shortening the clip by speeding it up will leave gaps.

Once you've applied a retiming effect, you can click and drag the two black bars at the edge of the gold timing bar above the clip to increase or decrease the percentage as well.

To create varying speeds within a clip, click on the retiming menu and then click **Speed Ramp.** This will divide your clip into four zones, which you can edit individually. The **To 0** speed ramp choice will cause your clip's speed to gradually fall from 100% to zero over the duration of the clip.

Screenshot 62: Speed Ramp

However, since you can change each segment of the ramp, you can actually speed your clip up and slow it down in each of the four segments if you like.

Another and more precise method for changing the timing of a specific portion of the clip is to use the Range Selection ® tool. Select a range and then use the retiming menu to adjust as needed.

4.6 Transforming, Cropping and Distorting Shots

FCPX includes several transformation features, which can be accessed using the button in the lower left corner of the Viewer window.

Screenshot 63: Transformation Features

Transform

Here you can rescale your image, which can function as a crop or a zoom. You can also rotate the clip and reposition it.

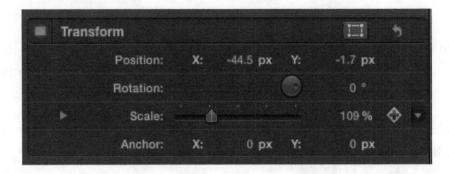

Screenshot 64: Transform

Split Screens

To create a split screen view (where more than one clip is playing on the screen at a time), stack your clips on top of each other in the Timeline. Then, use the scale and position tools to resize each clip window until it appears on the screen the way you want it to.

Crop

FCPX includes three crop settings – trim, crop and Ken Burns. Trimming a shot will reveal either the clip underneath it on the Timeline or empty black space. Cropping, on the other hand, will crop the footage and resize it so that it fills the screen. You can trim a shot into any proportion, but the crop tool enforces the video's aspect ratio. The Ken Burns setting is the zooming out while panning effect that lovers of the famous documentarian will immediately recognize. When the Ken Burns effect is active, the green rectangle represents the starting frame, and the red rectangle represents the finished frame. Position both frames and click **Done** to see the slow zoom-out effect in action.

Screenshot 65: Setting up the Ken Burns Effect

Distort

Distorting video can make for some fun special effects, but be on your guard against unintended cheesiness. Look under the **Distort** heading in the video tab of the Inspector window and adjust each corner to stretch and warp your shot, or use the blue handles in the Viewer window that become active when the distort tool is selected in the lower left corner of the Viewer.

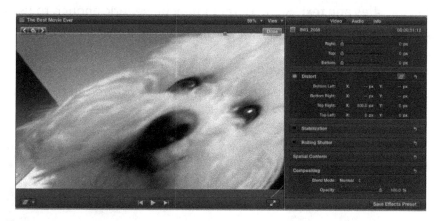

Screenshot 66: Distorting a Shot

4.7 Adding iPhoto / Photos and iMovie Files

As an Apple product, FCPX plays very nicely with Apple's photo and basic video manager apps iPhoto/Photos and iMovie. To access your iMovie and iPhoto/Photos libraries, click the camera icon. Apple discontinued iPhoto in 2015 in favor of its iOS-turned-desktop Photos app, but many users may still be running legacy versions of iPhoto. Don't worry – they behave almost identically! The contents of these libraries can be dragged and dropped into the Timeline. It's a great way to quickly add video or still images from your iPhone or iPad without needing to go through the steps of importing it.

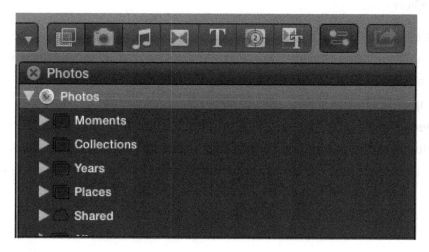

Screenshot 67: Accessing iPhoto/Photos Libraries

4.8 Video Generators

The icon to the right of the Text icon – Generators - contains several images that may be useful for creating backgrounds for titles and text. Some of them may be generic enough to use occasionally in your project, if you need a basic shot of clouds or an underwater scene, for example.

The placeholder generator can even allow you to do a limited amount of story boarding. This generator can be found in the **Elements** category, and it can be somewhat customized to suit your hypothetical scene.

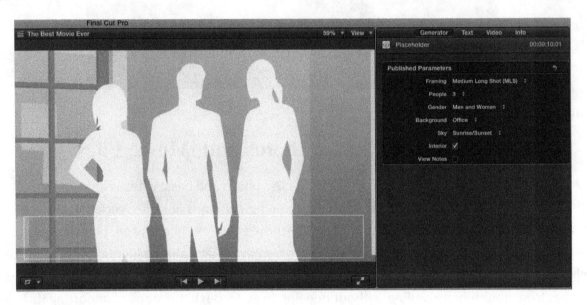

Screenshot 68: Placeholder Generator

Generators can be especially useful if you're working with green screen shooting. You can save an image as a background and then replace the green screen with that image to put your actors in your scene. To take advantage of this, you'll set up a background underneath your actors on the Timeline. Then, apply a keying effect to the actors' clips to allow the background to show through. The Luma Keyer effect is especially useful for green screen situations, since it works by replacing anything with a particular color value with the underlying background image. In the screenshot below, we've applied it to our placeholder in order to put our three characters in the clouds, courtesy of the clouds background.

Screenshot 69: Keying Effects

Note that Apple's animation software platform Motion (see 6.1) is a great tool for developing custom animated backgrounds that can be imported into FCPX.

4.9 Themes

The Themes browser gives you sets of visual extras (titles, transitions, and backgrounds) that work well together for a particular style. For example, the comic book theme pulls together elements that you'd expect in a comic book movie.

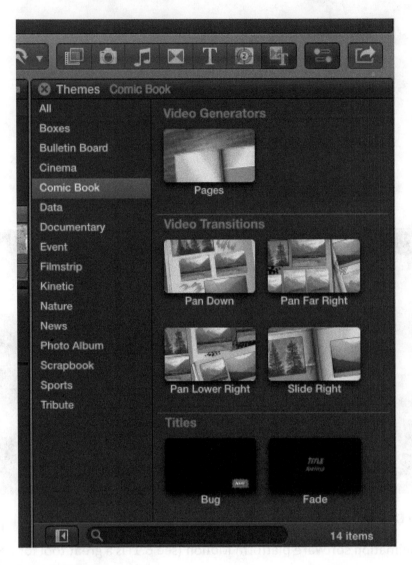

Screenshot 70: The Comic Book Theme

Select a category on the left and then drag and drop the generators, transitions, titles and / or effects as needed.

4.10 Freeze Frames and Stills

To freeze a frame from a clip in your library, find the frame and be sure the playhead is positioned over it in the Browser. Then click **Edit > Connect Freeze Frame** or press OPTION + F. This will add that frozen frame as a connected clip to the end of your project. You can also move the playhead over a frame on your Timeline and press OPTION + F to add a freeze frame to your primary storyline. Note that the **Hold** function in the Retiming menu can also be used to create a freeze frame.

You can also add still images to your FCPX library and projects. By default, your stills will be inserted into the Timeline with a duration of four seconds. When working with still images, FCPX will fit the image into the correct aspect ratio. However, this may result in unwanted black space. You can adjust this in the Viewer window by clicking **Fit** in the top right corner of the Inspector and choosing a percentage. Then, you can drag the red box inside the rectangle that appears along the right edge of the Viewer to move around the image and find the portion of it that looks the best in your project.

Screenshot 71: Adjusting Fit and Position of a Still Image

In the Inspector, you can also change the **Spatial Conform** of the image from Fit to Fill, which will allow FCPX to zoom in or out on your images automatically. Images can be transformed and distorted just like video can. You'll also find the Ken Burns effect with the image transform options, which will allow you to start zoomed in on a portion of your image and then zoom out to see the whole picture.

Screenshot 72: The Ken Burns Effect

4.11 Copying and Pasting Effects

When you add many kinds of effects – including color corrections (5.3) and transformations (4.6) – you may find that you need a quick way to apply them to a large number of clips to maintain visual consistency. The way to do this is through a pair of familiar keyboard shortcuts. Select the clip in the Timeline whose effects you need to copy. Press COMMAND + C. Then, select the clip or clips that you want to paste the effects onto and press COMMAND + OPTION + V. For the record, plain ol' COMMAND + V will paste the entire clip, along with its effects.

You can also paste selective effects and attributes of a clip by pressing COMMAND + SHIFT + V. This will bring up a window containing all of the attributes of your copied clip. You can then choose which ones you want to paste by clicking them.

Chapter 5: Advanced Editing

In this chapter, we're going to take a closer look at some more advanced editing tools and functions. The features we've covered so far are fine for simple projects, but you may get to a point in your creative career where you want to take things up a notch. Fortunately, FCPX offers plenty more beyond the basics.

5.1 Connected Clips, Secondary Story Lines and Compound Clips

In Final Cut Pro X, you can add additional timelines featuring supporting footage above your primary storyline. Think of the primary storyline as your main story, with additional time lines providing context, visual interest, etc.

To add this kind of footage, you'll use an **Add to Storyline** edit. Use the **Add to Storyline** button or press **Q** to add a "connected clip." This will place the clip above your primary storyline at the playhead's current location. As the playhead moves across the storyline, the connected clip will play on top of the primary storyline.

Your connected clip will stay tied to its current primary storyline footage, even if you move the primary clip. It will also be deleted if you delete your primary clip. However, you can manually adjust the connected clip's location by dragging it along the primary storyline. When you drop it, a new connection anchor will be created for you.

Working with connected clips is quite different than working with clips on your primary storyline. Your clips are a lot more gracious when trimming on the primary storyline, but if two connected clips run over each other, you'll notice some layering happening above your primary storyline. This happens because connected clips are connected at certain anchor points to the primary storyline and will maintain that connection point, even if it causes conflict between two connected clips.

Screenshot 73: Two Layers of Connected Clips

If you need to trim your connected clips, you won't be able to do a roll edit. You can perform a slip edit, but not a slide edit. However, it is possible to set up your connected clips so that they're a little more flexible by adding secondary storylines.

Secondary Storylines

If you have several connected clips side-by-side, you may have an easier time working with them if you convert them to a secondary storyline. Doing this restores the basic edits (roll and slide) that you cannot perform on connected clips.

To convert connected clips to a secondary storyline, click on them to select them, and then press COMMAND + G or click **Clips > Create Storyline.**

Screenshot 74: A Secondary Storyline

Once you've created a secondary storyline, your selected clips will appear inside a dark box. This box is connected to your primary storyline at its beginning, but the individual clip connection points are now gone. If you move the primary clip connected to the beginning of the secondary storyline, the entire secondary storyline will move with it. Otherwise, you're free to edit the clips within the secondary storyline just as you would footage in the primary storyline. You can swap shots and perform ripple, roll, slip and slide edits.

You can always select the secondary storyline and click **Clips > Break Apart Clip Items** if you'd like to return to a connected clips setup.

Compound Clips

Once you've added multiple storylines and audio tracks, you may find that the Timeline is getting a bit messy. To cut down on clutter, you can select related clips, right click the group, and then click **Create Compound Clip** or press OPTION + G. This will collapse the clips into one thumbnail to simplify the display. Compound clips can be moved and receive effects as a single unit.

Compound clips are *not* truly merged. You can break them up into their original elements easily by double clicking the compound clip.

5.2 Keyframes

If you want to apply an effect to a part of a clip or cause an effect to change over time, you can do so using keyframes. Keyframes are points within a clip that you can treat as a mini clip. They're also a key tool for animators. When you add keyframes to a clip, you add two points for the intensity or duration of an effect to move between. In other words, keyframes allow you to animate your effects.

To add keyframes, click the keyframe icon next to the effect's name in the Inspector – the diamond with a plus sign on it. Once you've added the keyframe, adjust all effects so that they appear as you want the beginning of the keyframed segment to appear.

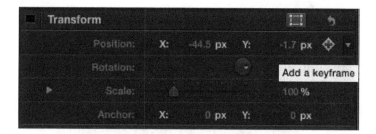

Screenshot 75: Add a Keyframe Button

Then, add another keyframe at the end of the segment, and adjust attributes to represent where you want the effect change to end up.

To take a look at how effects are working between two keyframes, right click the clip and then click **Show Video Animation.** This will bring up a list of the effects in play between the two keyframes.

Screenshot 76: Expanded Keyframe Animation

Each attribute can be expanded and adjusted here as needed.

5.3 Color Corrections

Color correction is an essential part of editing video, and FCPX offers several tools that make it simple and fun to undertake. For starters, the Enhancements menu gives you several easy post-processing tools that will help you make your shots stand out. You'll find this menu toward the right edge of the screen represented by a magic wand.

Screenshot 77: The Enhancements Menu

The first three tools here will help you adjust the color of your shots. Clicking **Show Color Board** will cause the color board to appear in the Inspector panel in the top right corner. Here, you can adjust the shadows, mid-tones and highlights of your shot, or adjust its saturation or exposure.

Screenshot 78: Color Board

You can correct the shot's color by sliding the dots up and down and left and right with the mouse or with the arrow keys (we find the arrow keys to be more precise). This is a great way to subtly adjust the warmth of a shot, as seen below:

Screenshot 79: Slight Color Corrections to Warm Up a Shot

Of course, this is also a gateway for much less subtle adjustments as well!

Screenshot 80: Extreme Color Correction

You can save color correction configurations as presets, which is a great idea if you'll be using similar effects throughout your project. Click the **Presets** button at the bottom right of the color board panel and then click **Save Preset** to name and save your current color configuration. You'll notice that FCPX includes several built-in presets that work like Instagram filters or Photoshop filters. They're an easy and fun way to completely restyle your shot with a single click.

Screenshot 81: Color Presets

The Saturation tab at the top of the Color Board gives you the ability to saturate and desaturate your footage for an artsy look. Upping the saturation, on the other hand, will give you a more vibrant look.

Screenshot 82: Saturation Changes

The Exposure tab will give you tools to play with the shot's exposure, which translates loosely to brightness. By playing with the shadows and highlights, you can achieve some unusual effects.

Screenshot 83: Exposure

Secondary Color Correction

Secondary color correction allows you to isolate and adjust hues in your shots. To do this, add a new color correction to the clip in question. Then, click the **Mask** button to the right of the color correction effect label and click **Add Color Mask.**

Screenshot 84: Color Correction Mask Button

This will change your cursor into an eyedropper. Use it to select a color from your shot that you'd like to edit. Once your color is selected, you can then go into the color board to selectively adjust that hue.

Bear in mind that isolating a hue doesn't isolate a part of the image. If you need to edit a hue in a specific part of a shot, then you'll need to create a shape mask. Click the mask button again, but this time click **Add Shape Mask.** This will allow you to position an oval around the area of the shot you want to adjust. You can then add a color mask to the shape to alter that particular area. This is a great way to subtly – or not so subtly – emphasize an element of your shot.

Screenshot 85: Using a Shape Mask for Color Correction

Canceling Changes

It's fun to play with color, saturation and exposure, but it's also pretty easy to get too far into left field! It's simple to remove a color configuration, though. Click the small arrow in the top right corner of the color board panel to return to the Inspector. Then, click the arrow next to **Color Correction 1** and click **Reset Parameter** to remove the effects. To turn off the effect without removing it entirely, click the blue box next to **Color Correction 1** to hide it. Click the box again to show it.

Correcting Color Cast

Colorcast refers to an unintended tinted appearance of a portion of your footage. It's something you'll find yourself correcting time and time again. Fortunately, FCPX can neutralize any unwanted color cast for you without much fuss. Just click **Balance Color** in the Enhancements menu.

5.4 Working with Audio

FCPX provides quite a few easy-to-use tools for making your audio sound great. Most of these adjustments take place inside the audio tab in the Inspector window. To reveal it, select an audio element on your Timeline. You may also want to toggle the Audio Meter on by clicking the two vertical bars next to the meter in the middle of the FCPX interface. This will show the audio meter in the lower right corner.

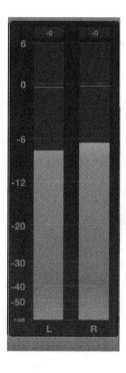

Screenshot 86: Audio Meter

When you start editing your audio, you'll find it much easier to work with one clip at a time. You'll need to "solo" each clip to work on it. Press OPTION + S or click the solo icon on the right above the Timeline. Notice that after you click this button, every other clip will be grayed out and you can work on the audio exclusively in your selected clip.

Screenshot 87: Solo Button

Adjusting Clip Volume

In the Inspector, use the loudness slider to adjust the volume of a clip. This is especially useful when you're working with multiple audio clips. For example, narration from the primary storyline may play over background noise from the secondary storyline. Moving audio levels up and down can help keep things consistent and easy to understand.

Handling Multiple Audio Channels

If you've shot a scene or recorded a clip using more than one audio channel, it won't be displayed on the Timeline itself by default. However, in the Audio Inspector under **Channel Configuration,** you can turn selected channels off and on. If you'd like to view multiple channels on the Timeline, right click the audio track and click **Expand Audio Components.** Doing this will also give you the ability to adjust each channel individually.

Removing Background Noise

Removing background noise is a basic and easy enhancement. To get to it, click the arrow next to **Audio Analysis** under the **Audio Enhancements** heading in the Inspector. This will reveal the Audio Enhancements panel.

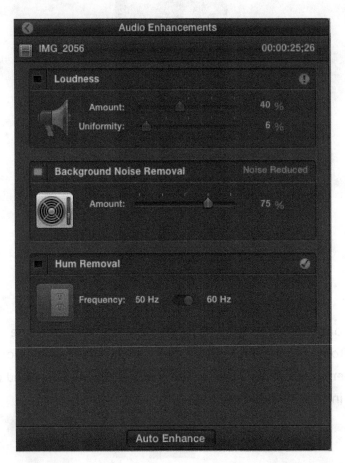

Screenshot 88: Audio Enhancements

Here, you can adjust not only the background noise levels, but also the overall volume and hum removal. There's also an **Auto Enhance** button at the bottom of the panel. Clicking that will allow FCPX to analyze and correct your audio for you.

Audio Equalization

FCPX includes a number of equalization filters that you can apply to your audio clips. You'll find them in the Audio Inspector under Audio Enhancements. Particularly useful settings here include Voice and Music Enhance.

Screenshot 89: Audio Equalization

Audio equalization works by emphasizing designated audio frequencies. For example, boosting the bass means turning up the volume on lower frequencies so that the beat really grinds. Similarly, Voice Enhance turns up the frequencies of the human voice, making it easier to hear and understand speech. You can check out what frequencies each equalization option affects by clicking the tiny square next to the Equalization selection in the Audio Inspector. This will reveal the Graphic Equalizer.

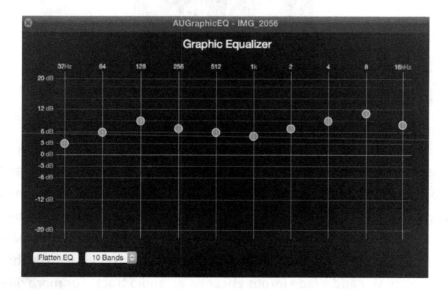

Screenshot 90: Graphic Equalizer

This graph can be edited. Just drag each point up or down with your mouse to adjust each frequency. This is both an art and a science, and it's well worth your time to explore the possibilities here!

Fading In/Out

To fade audio in, add an audio track to the Timeline. You'll see a very small circle at the very beginning of the green audio track bar. Drag that circle toward the right to create a fade-in effect. As you drag, you'll see a dark curve appear on the audio track. The end point of that curve represents the moment when the music will reach full volume.

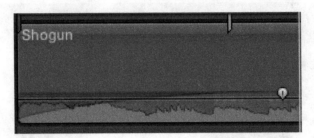

Screenshot 91: Fading in Audio

You can also raise and lower the audio track's volume throughout the clip. The easiest way to do this is using the Range Selection tool. Use range selection to select the section of audio you want to manipulate. After you've made your selection, move your cursor to the black bar in the middle of the track. This represents the baseline volume. Dragging your cursor up will cause the audio volume to increase, and dragging it down will cause a decrease. If you look closely at the baseline volume, you'll see that FCPX will automatically transition into the lower or higher range, smoothing out the effect by inserting keyframes at the beginning and end of the range.

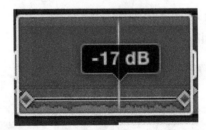

Screenshot 92: Adjusting the Volume of a Range of Audio

Audio Keyframes

If you need to adjust the audio within a clip, you can do this by adding keyframes in addition to using range selection. To insert a keyframe, press OPTION + CLICK. You'll see that a diamond appears next to your cursor. Once you see the diamond, click on the audio track twice – once at the beginning of the section you need to edit and once at the end. From there, you can drag the centerline up and down to adjust the audio for the keyframed segment of the clip. Note that this is essentially the same thing that FCPX inserts for you when you add a fade in/out effect on an audio track. For more on keyframes, see 5.2.

Recording Audio

You can actually record audio directly in FCPX. To do so, click **Window > Record Voiceover.** Then click the red button to start recording.

Screenshot 93: Audio Recording

The recording will be inserted wherever your playhead is currently located, but once it appears on your Timeline, you can move it and adjust it as needed.

5.5 Markers

Markers are an extremely useful way to leave notes for yourself or for your colleagues that are connected to a very specific frame of your project. Markers appear just above the Timeline as little colored marks.

To add a marker, just press M with the playhead located at the position you want the marker to appear at. To add a note to the marker, press M again (or press OPTION M to get straight to the dialog box).

Screenshot 94: Adding a Marker with a Note

In the Marker dialogue box, you can add a simple note (shown above), or you can add a task by clicking the middle icon at the top of the dialog box. The bookmark icon will let you add a chapter heading, which is useful when packaging a project for release.

To view Marker notes and tasks, double click the marker. To view all markers associated with a project, use the Timeline Index. Click **Tags** at the top, and then click the Marker icon at the bottom.

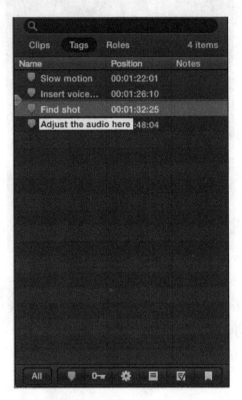

Screenshot 95: Markers in the Timeline Index

If you've added Markers as tasks, you'll use the Tasks icon instead. Completed Tasks will appear under the task icon with a checkmark.

5.6 Working with Multiple Cameras

FCPX makes it very easy to work with multiple camera angles through multicam group clips. There is a little bit of setup required to get this to work. Basically, you need to sync related clips so that you can confidently switch angles at precise moments in your project's time.

The easiest and quickest way to sync multiple camera angles is through audio synchronization. This analyzes clips to determine how to sync them up by matching their audio waveforms. Of course, the catch here is that in order for this to work, every camera has to be recording audio!

To group your angles into one clip, select each shot and then right click the group. Then, click **New Multicam Clip.** Be sure that **Use Audio for Synchronization** is checked. Click **OK.** Your new multicam clip will then be available for use in your project.

If the audio method won't work for your angle group, click **Custom Settings** on the New Multicam Clip creation box. This will give you other points of reference for the synchronization operation, including time code. You can also use markers to indicate the points at which you'd like the sync to start on each angle. Beware, though – this requires immense patience and precision!

To view all of the angles in a multicam clip, click **Window > Viewer Display > Show Angles.** To switch between camera angles, click on each angle that you'd like to switch to in the Inspector.

Once you've got a rough edit of your multicam clip, you can right click on individual segments and change the camera angle. You can also select a clip and open the Angles Viewer and press OPTION+CLICK on the angle you want to use.

You can roll edit between angle switches just like you can between main clips. Unlike main clips, FCPX will default to a roll edit when working inside multicam clips.

5.7 Try it out!

At this point, you have a solid handle on the basic and not-so-basic components of the FCPX software. Of course, there's much more to video editing than knowing where to click. We strongly encourage you to experiment with each feature described in this guide. Trust your own eyes and instincts, and you'll soon find your own editorial voice. The only way to develop that voice, though, is through experimentation and experience. Have fun and don't be afraid to try unexpected configurations and unfamiliar adjustments!

Chapter 6: FCPX and Beyond

Like other professional editing platforms, FCPX is open to plugins and downloads that can greatly enhance your ability to produce great work. Apple also offers several pieces of software that work extremely well with FCPX. In this chapter, we'll give you an introductory tour of some of the resources and supporting applications that can greatly extend FCPX's functionality. Apple also maintains a list of FCPX apps and plugins at https://www.apple.com/final-cut-pro/resources/ecosystem.html

6.1 Apple Motion 5 ($49.99)

Apple Motion 5 is animation software that works extremely well with FCPX. Motion is great for creating 3D titles and animations. It looks and feels very similar to FCPX, and it's easy to export Motion animations for use inside your FCPX projects. Motion includes the ability to create animated 3D text from scratch and to create 3D titles from 2D text. It also really shines as a text manipulator and credit sequence designer. Like FCPX, Motion includes generators and other presets that make creating beautiful moving graphics easy and fun. You can also open FCPX generators and themes in Motion to customize them further. If you need a specific kind of generator, for example, Motion is an excellent tool for creating an animated background.

There's a lot to Motion, but if you have any use for animation in your FCPX projects, it's well worth the price. With a solid foundation in FCPX's interface, you'll be able to learn and use Motion fairly easily.

6.2 Apple Compressor 4 ($49.99)

Apple Compressor 4 is a tool for custom encoding. This is useful for FCPX users who need a little help sticking the landing on their export process. You can encode closed-captioning files, keywords and other metadata along with your project by using Compressor.

Compressor also makes it much, much easier to export your FCPX projects into common formats. For example, you can optimize a project for Facebook, Vimeo or other web services. You could also create a Blu-Ray disc or export your project for use on a member of the Apple device family.

Of course, FCPX itself is capable of most basic exporting operations. Compressor really starts shining though when you start exporting files in bulk. It gives you a lot of flexibility and tools for batch processing by allowing you to send multiple projects for export at once. Compressor also makes the process of creating an Apple-compliant iTunes submission easy, which is an excellent perk if you plan to sell your creations in iTunes.

6.3 Third Party Plugins

Like many other popular applications Final Cut Pro X allows you to install plugins made by other people. Final Cut Pro X plugins generally allow for added functionality, or simplification of complex tasks. There are hundreds, if not thousands, of plugins that allow for new transitions between clips that allow for new title sequences, that apply various color effects to clips, or that provide video templates for showing more than one clip at a time.

Many of the high-end most complex plugins cost money, but there are certainly free plug-ins available that can really liven up your video! In this section we'll take a look at some of the

Paid Plugin Sources

FCPeffects

FCPeffects (found at www.fcpeffects.com) is one of the biggest names in Final Cut Pro X plugins and they offer a wide variety of paid options that can really overhaul your video projects.

Screen Splitter 2 by FCPeffects is one of the most versatile template plugins available. It offers 123 different split screen effects, each of which is customizable by size, giving you thousands of different possibilities to show multiple clips at the same time.

FCPeffects' **Advanced Masking Tools** expands on the masking tools already available in Final Cut Pro, and simplifies a lot of common tasks related to masking, such as blurring the background behind a subject in a video. It also comes with more default options than are available natively in FCPX by offering simpler controls and more options for mask points. This is definitely a time saver for anything masking-related.

Organic Light Leaks is another plugin available from FCPeffects that provides a transition based on a "light leak" effect. This transition, which is similar to a lens flare, was popularized in the latest Star Trek movies, and now you can also achieve this effect in your own transitions. The plug in contains over 150 light leaks that are each customizable to help you get exactly the right look for your transition.

The **Finishing Plugin** by FCPeffects is a powerful tool that allows you to make your videos really pop - even if your clips were shot on less than ideal equipment. Using this tool you can quickly and easily enhance the vibrancy and sharpness of your clips as well as recover fine details lost due to camera quality. The Finishing Plugin provides a great "last step" in your editing that will make your video look professional and sharp.

FCPeffects offers numerous other plugins that can apply customized templates, transitions and effects that will help you to take your videos to the next level and simplify your editing process. Make sure to check out what they have to offer at www.fcpeffects.com.

Motionvfx

Motionvfx is another big name in paid Final Cut Pro X plugins and features a number of dramatic options for your video project. Check out their wide product line at www.motionvfx.com.

Their latest plugin at the time of this writing is called **mVolumetric**, a plugin that adds volumetric light rays on top of your clip. The light rays are customizable so you can set areas that would block the light ray, or set, in three dimensions, how the light behaves and what the source of the light is. Though creating your own realistic light rays might require some practice, Motionvfx also bundles this plugin with 30 free templates to get you started and that feature pre-created title scenes, effects and transitions.

Also by Motionvfx is **mTitle 3D**. This plugin is a set of 31 3D title sequences that can take your title sequence to a professional level in just a few clicks. The 31 different title presets have titles like Tonight Show, Grunge, and Sport, and there's a suitable 3D title set for just about any type of video. This versatile plugin is a must-have for any aspiring video editor!

The **mTransition Simple** pack by Motionvfx is a set of 50 additional transitions for FCPX. Used just like the transitions that come with FCPX, these simple transitions will greatly expand the basic transitions available to you. For even more dramatic transitions, Motionvfx also offers the **mTransition Light** plugin that features light-based transitions, such as a spotlight moving across the screen. Many of these transitions are also available with the much larger mVolumetric plugin described above.

Motionvfx offers many more plugins for a variety of purposes that can add professional looking effects, transitions and title sequences to your project. Make sure to check them out at www.motionvfx.com to see everything they have to offer!

Free plugins

Though FCPeffects and Motionvfx offer robust paid plugins, there are also lots of resources for free plugins on the web as well that can be found using simple web searches. In this section we'll look at some of the coolest free plugins from the web.

Text Colour Split by Idustrial Revolution is a simple, free animated title template plugin that horizontally splits the screen into two areas of editor specified colors, and then applies the text along the split creating a two toned appearance. It's definitely worth adding this title template to your repertoire! Text Colour Split and many other incredible plugins can be found at www.idustrialrevolution.com.

Video in Text by Ripple Training is another free title template for FCPX. This plugin inverts the traditional title template where rather than applying a title on top of a clip, the clip is visible inside the letters of the title (written in a large, bold font) with a neutral background behind the text. This plug-in might not work well for lengthy titles but, with a short title, this plugin can create a really dramatic effect. The Video in Text plugin is available for free on the Ripple Training website: www.rippletraining.com.

Transition Love Lite is a free plugin set from the blog lightleaklove.com (which itself is a great resource for learning to edit video in FCPX). Similar to the mTransition Light and the Organic Light Leaks plugins listed above, the Transition Love Light plugin allows you to add a transition that creates a light leak. Though it comes with fewer presets and customizations than the paid plugin, it's definitely a useful plugin to have at a great price! Transition Love Lite is available on the www.lightleaklove.com website along with the full (paid) version, Transition Love Collection.

Alex4d is a huge contributor to the Final Cut Pro X community and often releases his own plugins—for free. One of his free offerings that is very useful for many projects is his **Flashback** transition, which he describes as a "'Scooby Doo' flashback effect." This is the ideal plugin to apply at a jump where someone is experiencing a flashback to the past! Check out that plugin, and all of Alex4D's wonderful creations, at his website www.alex4d.com.

The Final Cut King is a great resource for learning about digital video editing and offers his free **Tilt Shift Effect** plugin for FCPX. This plugin creates a tilt shift effect over a clip. The tilt shift effect is a popular effect used on large environmental shots and makes scenes look as though they are being viewed in miniature, almost as though you are looking down at a scale replica of the setting. This can be a difficult effect to create by hand, but it becomes a snap when using this plugin. It's available on the Final Cut King website at www.finalcutking.com.

Finally, Crumblepop, amongst their numerous paid plugins offers a free effect plugin called **Noir Moderne Light**. This plugin applies a grayscale filter and generates some film grain and vignette effects to give your clip a "noir" feel. It comes with three built in presets and one free noir-inspired font. This plugin is great for lots of situations and is available at the Crumblepop website alongside many useful paid plugins at www.crumblepop.com.

Conclusion

We hope you've enjoyed learning the ins and outs of Final Cut Pro X! You now know how to find your way around the FCPX interface, manipulate your footage by inserting and trimming it on the Magnetic Timeline, apply titles, transitions, effects and transformations, work with several advanced tools to produce professional-caliber video projects, and seek out plugins and applications that further extend FCPX's functionality.

Of course, this is only the beginning. Now that you've got the tools, it's up to you to provide the artistry! FCPX provides the full technical platform you need to realize your vision, and we wish you the best with all of your video editing endeavors.

www.ingramcontent.com/pod-product-compliance
Lightning Source LLC
Chambersburg PA
CBHW060458060326
40689CB00020B/4575